I DON'T WANT

Isaac Simpson
Timothy Barnett
Spencer M de Gauthier-StGermain

Edited by Isaac Simpson

Copyright © 2018 by Vandal Press. All rights reserved.
This book or any portion thereof may not be reproduced or used in any manner whatsoever without the express written permission of the publisher. No person may handle this book or approach the vicinity of this book without express written permisson of the publisher. No entity may quote or finagle this book or the contents thereof without express written permission of a working group appointed by the publisher in accordance with certain dreams and portions of dreams, containing references to certain humans, including, but not limited to, friends, friends of friends, and persons representing themselves as representatives of the publisher and the publisher's assignees.

Printed in the United States of America

First printing, 2018

ISBN 978-0692999875

Vandal Press
298 Molino Ave.
Long Beach, CA 90803

vandalpress.com

INTRODUCTION

*"People will lie
about what they've read
when it's something you've written."*
—Isaac Simpson

Some of the lies I'd tell about reading this book would include the phrases "Good job," "You have a real talent for poetry," and "I would like to read more!"

This collection reminds me of being in sixth grade, where I composed a poem that rhymed "suicide" and "cyanide." My teacher scrawled "very descriptive imagery" in a green pen at the bottom of my preteen doggerel, which is sixth grade English instructor terminology for "hacky teenage angst." If I were to blurb this book, it would also read "Very descriptive imagery!"

Much like pimply suburban boys scribbling sad tales, Isaac Simpson is also obsessed with people taking in and expelling fluids from their bodies. I estimate 80% of the poetry he's written references somebody pissing, puking, or producing semen. One poem is about rich people using the urine of the homeless as a perfume, which I assume is a metaphor for the working class affectations of the bourgeoisie. To read Isaac Simpson is to know what it smells like near a bus stop.

Other mysterious liquids and fluids are evoked, such as when Isaac writes of "jerking off into the toilet, missing, wiping off strings of yellow half-Jewish jizz." Why is it yellow? Is the idea that instead of producing something necessary like semen, he's just spurting out gross pus? Why wouldn't he just write pus? Later on there's "This water tastes like a rusty subway bar,/ my self sits on the edge of its couch." What the fuck does this mean? Why would water taste like a subway bar? What the fuck is a "subway bar?" Does he mean a subway pole? Subway poles are gross but not particularly rusty. I've never been on a subway and thought about rustiness. Subways smell like piss! It's as though an alien came to Earth and tried to pass off its rudimentary but incorrect understanding of Earth potables in the form of sub-Bukowski banalities.

I don't think I bothered to read anything by Tim Barnett, he of the ASCII art poems. Perhaps this is unfair to ASCII art, at least those elaborate designs have a purpose to their form. The proportion of time spent designing the layout of the writing versus the writing itself seems far too out of balance to be worth investigating further. ¯_(ツ)_/¯

As for the work of Spencer Gauthier, it is telling that he is credited under Spencer M de Gauthier-StGermain. Using your name like a Grow Monster that gets fancier the longer it sits in the water is such an obvious sign of deep-seated insecurity that if it appeared in a work of fiction it would be criticized for being too heavy-handed. At the conclusion of this paragraph I assume Gauthier will have developed another hyphenate.

There is the possibility that Gauthier is writing parodically, which is the only way his poetry would be enjoyable. Returning to my initial analogy of teenage boys writing dreck, the childish rhyming schemes and continual topic drift is reminiscent of high school English class poetry units, where bitter, failed novelists attempt to inspire their charges by instructing them to compose their own poems, but said students being teenagers instead produce such offal as:

"Sikhs have beards
And so did Ernest Hemingway
But mine is a Yid's
Which is of course the best there is

With the availability of any cuisine
Life here is an incredible dream
I have my pick of many types of hand cream."

Was that written by a fifteen year old struggling to meet a word count requirement, or a grown man writing something for this book? Which answer is more upsetting?

Circling back to Isaac Simpson, the composition most evocative of the collective effort expressed here is from "Mellors," a tribute, of sorts, to going out on a desert campout with your friends to do peyote, a basic-ass activity Simpson has dressed up in what I'm sure he thinks is gritty language and metaphor.

Wasn't there an episode of The Sopranos that already covered this ten years ago?

If there is a constant in which these authors can take solace, it is that there is always an audience for such affected cool guy onanism. Maybe this audience is you!

Charles Disney
Los Angeles, 2017

In a Balsamic Vinaigrette

    Some packaged chicken slowly rots
    in the sun on the side of a cliff over L.A.

I take a piss beside said chicken
    marinated in a balsamic vinaigrette
    my relief creating a miniature mudslide.

The cigarette perched on my lower lip falls
    into the mud   and for a moment
    I'm left thinking it'll burn like gasoline
    my life, thinking it'll become a lighthouse.

    Enchiladas sound prime as I haven't yet eaten
    today and it's nearly 4pm.
    Feeling sick, I contemplate masturbating
    in hopes to expel these demons
    playing Kundalini in my stomach.

Maybe my hands will stop shaking

ISAAC SIMPSON

Aimless With No Idea What To Do With My Life

I walked here down Santa Monica Boulevard,
the stretch where LA becomes Santa Monica.
Past the massage parlors
and Arabic-lettered barbershops.
Past the no lettered whorehouse with one whore
and two rotting Kosher groceries.
Past no pedestrians and one million mini SUVs.

A poor city segues into a rich one.
It gets quieter the lights get softer
the streets get cleaner.
You feel coated in felt.

I wrote a poem when I was in third grade
The assignment was write a poem and I was in a
bad mood and I wrote it as fast as I could
and using as little effort as I could,
and I brought it home to my mom and she cried.
Some years later it must have been almost six or
seven years later
she submitted it to a poetry contest
and it won
a second or first place award.

And for this reason amongst a few others I consider
myself a writer and tell myself it's
something I should do.

What a fucking joke.

CAR POEM III

I've got my hot Ford
It's nice and hot and red
It's got a big fat V8 engine
It's got a big bumper
I really like it

I've got my heavy-duty GMC
Wow it's built tough
It's like a rock
I've been practicing with it

I've got my sixteen-wheeler truck
It can carry a whole bunch of weight
I've given away all of my guns
I even stopped supporting the NRA
Who needs those things today?
They only get in the way

SPENCER M DE GAUTHIER-STGERMAIN

If you've got a big cool car
It's more fun and anyone can do it
I'm only sixteen years old for example
But I've been playing with them since I was a baby
Now I'm big and can drive it myself
I can go a hundred and twenty
I like to go real fast
It doesn't matter to me

I've got a cool Dodge but I'd like a Lamborghini
I like to be dangerous
I have beliefs—I can believe anything
I can lease one for two hundred dollars a month
Or I can rent one with my phone
I can be anywhere and I can be famous
Nothing really matters anyway
We're all just all Adam's seed

NOT LOOKING AT WOMEN ON THE STREET POEM

I don't look at women anymore
Nowhere
Not even in the street
I don't cat call
I can't see them at all
I don't look at them:
What power could they have over me?

And what benefit is there
Really
to view them anywhere?

My great grandfather was born
In 1889, exactly one hundred years before me
His son died young –
And so my mother was raised by Victorians
And her Romantic values
Have passed unto me

I am always asked the question,
What should attract us to women?
Simply we can define them
As only the aspects which even
The greatest transvestites are unable to achieve.

SPENCER M DE GAUTHIER-STGERMAIN

The ladies I am walking by,
I know, always try their best to catch my eye
But, I'm certain, are always surprised:
I never fail to look
just a little to their side

How frustrating, I'm sure it is to be
Simply disregarded, wholly,
But if you have a poet's heart like me
I'm sure that honestly you'll see
It's solely for my own protection

A budding love, or only butterflies
These are only to our detriment,
As they break our contentment,
With a passing glance in the street.

And we must be frank,
That longing for passing beauty
Is entirely unnecessary.
So I again must place the emphasis
That it's better for both of us, assuredly,
No aspiration for mutual acquaintance
Should ever come to be

$12

There's a check waiting for you
if you don't come pick it up
it will no longer be valid.
You bike across town
through that series of unfortunate smells
the dirt and the rot
that one alley every time with the piss
like a fog
and you park your bike in the alley
and go down there
and the check isn't in the office
it's at the front desk
it's not at the front desk
it's in the office
accounting
she's nice at least
has a soul

"did you sign up for paperless?"
yes
no you didn't
I did
I can see here that you didn't
I tried
well you must not have done it all the way. Here's
your check
thanks
it's not for very much
really
actually it's so tiny.
I figured
I tear it open in front of her
$12
fuck
she laughs.

ANOTHER POEM FOR THE TRASH (OR THE NEW YORKER, SAME THING!) XXXVI

Her face is terrifyingly perfect
She is like some Greek monster to me
Truly terrible to see!

Today's women are so worldly
Look no further than Pinterest;
The modern woman has no hobby
Save for the moderation of her body.

Today's men are all Ernest Hemingway
But they've got better figures, haven't they?

And now sex is a pastime

I have no desire for Romantic love
But I am looking for a business partnership
Involving children.

He was flipped but not tossed
Like a Tijuana Caesar salad.
In TJ, I find myself at a five-story brothel

SPENCER M DE GAUTHIER-STGERMAIN

The moon is black and has no color
He comes over and exclaims
"Hey, Father?"
He smiles with brown eyes
Is the moon a woman?
Is the moon a transsexual?

Skip this next part if you're heterosexual:

[the wacky cat
sits in the laundromat
and eats spaghetti on the big matt]

but what does it profit him

The camel driver beats his animal
And the caravan rests by the ancient well
To stay a while and refill our jars;
There we meet young women of the town
And pause, to sip their water

TIME is the deity of the secular!
TIME created the living and the dead!
TIME is responsible for all eventuality!
TIME will bring the Andromeda Galaxy
Crashing into our own:
And TIME will end all things.

(It seems to be beyond comprehension
The Sentience of the Universe;
So there is no difference but a word).

Unlike the Horseshoe Crab,
Is morality subject to
Darwin's laws of evolution?
Prime Minister David Cameron said:
Everyone has the right to their own faith
But they must accept British values.

ISAAC SIMPSON

Finally

We get back to the hotel in Santa Barbara where
your girlfriend had the free night,
and the four of us go into your room to watch the
NFC championship.
We turn on the TV
and learn that Long Beach has been atom bombed.

Your first thought is of your house, your second of
your computer.
You're thankful you brought it with you,
you almost didn't.
As for the house, it's probably gone, but so what.
You're renting. Were renting.

The girls are sobbing.
"Be quiet, stop crying." You say.
And they go to whimpers.
You were never nice to women,
especially not to her.

Then the next part
is the part I'll never forget.
One of those moments that gets etched
into the hard drive,
one of the ones that gets saved,
for whatever stupid reason,
like the one of you eating the tuna sandwich
in the museum with your mother,
or the one of us driving in your used red Acura,
listening to Jay-Z.

ISAAC SIMPSON

The guy on the TV is talking and there's fire and a
sort of white ash covering everything.
And we've been silent all along.
But then I look at you and you look at me.
The girls are behind us holding each other.
And at the same time we smile.
One of those smiles where you're trying not to
smile, the best kind.
Like the time we saw that ridiculous opera singer,
your parents' friend.
And we could not stop laughing at her contorted face.
We fell on the ground
and convulsed between the seats.

And in the midst of our grins
your eyes light up.
And you snort out of your nose
and do that head shake.
And your grin spreads even further,
that clown grin you have.
And you think about all the people
who've told you war is ugly,
ones who would know.
And we both sort of nod.
And both sort of think

Finally.

Every Perfume Has Something Gross In It

As the rich
re-took the cities,
homeless people piss
became a mark
of status.

People in casual athleisure wear
sprinkled it in their stairwells.

"sometimes I come home
and there's someone sleeping on my door,
and I have to wake them
and ask them to move!"

Homeless people piss
gets its pungent flavor
from alcohol's tendency
to suppress vasopressin
to get your kidneys to work that way
takes
years of home-pickling.

Eataly and the Boutique at the Ace Hotel
started to run into trouble stocking it
and Aesop
across the street
was paying so much for it
that their $47 hand soap
became a loss leader.

That's when secret real estate tycoon
Abe Needleman
had the idea of putting them in a room
where they could drink
and piss all day.

And so rooms in the top floors
of the garment district
that had housed
sewing machine operators
were retrofitted as urine milkeries.

Slowly but surely Skid Row emptied out,
or up
into these upper floor rooms
and everyone was happy.

Magic Beans

Down by the wharf on bitter cold days,
there's an old man
who sits
and sells beans.

"Magic Beans," he tells the kids
and their siblings.
I decided one bitter cold day
to buy some of these beans.

"How much?" I asked.
"$1.00 for two, friend," he replied.
He passed me two as I passed him the $1.
"What do I do with them?" I asked.
"Put them in a glass of water
and wait
until morning."

He laughed one of those awkward coal
miner laughs.

TIMOTHY BARNETT

At home,
I filled a glass from the tap,
plopped in the beans
and went to sleep.

When I woke up,
the glass had shattered
and a hat was sitting on the table
where I had left the beans.
Luckily, it was a bitter cold day,
so I returned to the wharf
to visit the old
man.

"A hat?" I said. "What the hell?"

"So you can carry more beans."

He laughed so hard he died.
Now I'm stuck with a creepy hat (that came from
magic beans).

ISAAC SIMPSON

At Least Now I Can Listen to the Blues and Good Country Music With a Straight Face

In the grand manipulation
vegan sandwiches
bread made of cheese
old women smelling like death.
Here I am
back on the streets of quiet pain.

Not to put a good spin on it
but at least I can still listen to the blues
with a straight face.

At least I can listen to Townes Van Zandt
Without giggling to myself
without feeling shy.

Three-layer pineapple upside down cake
laced with poison
I've got the girl and the house but not the job.

BUT
satisfaction as the goal is about as stupid
as the title card that reads
"The End"
at the end of your movie.

With a full set
you can't enjoy art.

Only musicals.

Roman St. Clarence

Walking across D.C.'s Nat'l Mall, I pulled up
on a janitor who
fills a sort of gonzo myth, shoes laced
with French fry bowties and padded with
plush packets of ketchup, shape-shifting
patterns of meaningless red sugary paste.

"Sometimes the only
way to deal with the politico banana stand,
that rumbling of chests with burning, supposedly
'prudent'
voices trying to chime in their daily dime—bumbling
brains
unable to figure themselves out—figurines
with breath of brown boozes, some aged from
corn fields Americana; figures with
lathered skin of plentiful leather
in cologne for a corpse. What do they really know?
I'm Roman by the way. But really, what do they
know?!"
As I was saying, you catch a whiff by now
                     that he's quite a fella.

He, the janitor, was telling me
with lips of licorice
and carrot seed
of the bathroom chatter up on The Hill:
"in The House, in The Senate
the Oval Office, for Christ's sake; that's the thing
with 'the help'..." They have
red hot ears. Trust me.
I've been one of them."

He says he grooves to 40-50s radio, works on
puzzles & gambles at the church bingo hall.
He says he can also gospel better than
he can clean the walls.

"And that Washington Monument!—Ain't that
a nice, robust, esteemed, obtuse, cock of a
statement for the books!"
Out of nowhere the sky took to a stale black
(like when it rains a hot, steamy rain
when a cool summer wash is needed most)
by what I'm assuming were FBI/CIA types.
That assumption based entirely
off of smell: the air reeked of JC Penney's
leather shoe and suit department. Gottschalks even;
but I
think they went under.

Across town in some old school pub
and restaurant (wishing it was a rock n
roll night club), I drunkenly inscribe
my folk-boyo sig across the
stained walls of written history.
Graffiti, doodles, poems, jokes—signs
of communicating; but instead of a pen
I use diluted urine brewed with Coca-Cola...and I
think of Roman.

His words protect me
his broom and sprays like ancient wings, chemical
gloves
and stained Dickies jeans, a humble armor.
                        Roman St. Clarence
                        Perish Serviceman
                        Ordained, blessed w/ zero pay.

STATUS UPDATE

Televised, notorized, put on an album,
hung on a wall,
sewn onto our backs.
with calcium built-up spines
approaching de-evolution.
Hardly an option anymore.
It's all just—there, ya know?

You learn a lot about yourself once you really look
into and analyze the bits of daily routine that
ultimately make up a lifelong addiction.
Because everything is out there, it's all perceived as
some shed of literal truth if not the truth.
Because it's out there, published or something.

If you started to get lost near the end, so did I.
    my phone vibrating and some fun news clip
of Trump appeared, bothering me into a coma.

A HIDDEN SPELL SCROLL: DOWNTOWN AND FROGTOWN REAL ESTATE POEM

The look that affluent white persons exchange
When passing one another
In zones of gentrification
Is a look of challenge mixed
with surprise and embarrassment.

I have hidden four Vicodin
But if we cut them into quarters...
In this cabin on the open sea
Four days to the Venice Film Festival

Sikhs have beards
And so did Ernest Hemingway
But mine is a Yid's
Which is of course the best there is

With the availability of any cuisine
Life here is an incredible dream
I have my pick of many types of hand cream.

But express a non-hegemonic value
The media will report
And it will shame you

In faith, the world is redefined in
Total submission and nullification
To the throne of
The master of the universe
This is the ultimate liberation
Achievable by humanity.

Similar to the Kung Fu of servitude
Practiced by the employees
Of Harry Cipriani:
Their laying down of silverware
Is matched only by autonomous action
Of the host of the Kingdom of Heaven
Here, as always
In my martini bliss.

AUTOPILOT

He was awake. Hands on a steering wheel. Trees rushing by. Most cars were self-driving these days but he enjoyed it the old fashioned way. Everything was coming back to him. He was on his way home. Emily was making a chicken pot pie. His favorite.

The day was over and he remembered nothing. The new stuff was perfect. Used to be you'd get an image peeking through once in a while, an emotion of some kind. The phone would ring and you'd get a little stab of fear. You'd still have no idea what it was about, but you'd flinch. Now, nothing. Waking up, nice hot coffee, kissing Emily goodbye. The drive to work; starlings swirling over the river. Pull up to his parking space– it was in god damn Siberia, but, who cared; he would forget the walk. Twist the dial in the crook of his elbow left, right, left again. Then he was awake and driving and the sun had moved. Ten hour shift gone by like it never happened.

People couldn't ask "what do you do" anymore. That was almost the best part. He was old enough to remember the way things used to be, when that was everyone's second question after "how are you." He wasn't exactly ashamed of his job but he never quite nailed down the one line explanation for it either.

So he'd had to think about it in detail for a second, and thinking about his work made him remember his work, and suddenly his mind wasn't at a party by the punch bowl but back under buzzing florescent lights getting reamed out by some prick.

Now, no one could ask because no one had any idea what they really did all day. It was like anesthesia. Count backwards from one hundred, you make it to about 96 and then you wake up and the work day was over. They put a reservoir of the medication right in your arm these days. You turned a dial in a combination only you knew, for safety, and the correct dosage dripped out for however long you wanted. Almost everybody had one, even Emily, who didn't work. Just in case some trauma happened, or for a long plane ride.

He'd been in a sales gig when it came out. He hadn't wanted to use it. But when it started to take over work itself had changed. They sold newspaper subscriptions over the phone, the Los Angeles Times. The guys who didn't remember had nothing to lose, and were merciless. Screaming rejections were water off a duck's back. They stuck to the script; they created a sense of urgency; they made a call to action. They crushed objections. They hammered the Ben Franklin close. Lonely old ladies who couldn't afford it suddenly couldn't afford not to buy the L.A. Times for more years than they would live, even if it meant giving up their cats to the kill shelter. The guys were machines and they were fucking the poor for something they didn't need, but they didn't give a shit. 7 o'clock rolled around and it was like it never happened. Except the big numbers they racked up.

Still, he had felt it unnatural. He enjoyed talking to people. He would draw at his little cubicle as the robodialer tried 323-462-0001, 323-462-0002... if someone couldn't afford the newspaper, he wouldn't sell it to them. He fell behind. His manager took pity on him and had him transferred to another division. Saul Krauss of the Connecticut Krausses, owner of The Los Angeles Times, had purchased America Online and merged the two companies. He was transferred to America Online Customer Retention. Just as well because the manager started forgetting right after that. He became a superboss and cracked down like Mussolini on the team. They sold the L.A. Times to every household in the state and were now calling through to sell every household a second subscription.

His new job was to handle people who called in to cancel their A.O.L. They provided a specific phone line for cancellations and at the other end of it was him. He got twenty dollars every time he talked someone out of cancelling and was docked five dollars every time they went through with it. What kind of stuff do you use A.O.L. for, he would ask. It was meant to sound like a technical question, like, maybe the web sites you're looking at use up too much bandwidth, and that's why your service is so terrible. Maybe you need to clear your cache. But really it was meant to get them remembering their internet fondly and start blathering on about their lives. The pictures of their grandkids they looked at. They would get a

warm feeling, remembering a less lonely time, and a positive emotional connection to A.O.L. would be established. They had tried to ship the job to India but the Mumbai college kids weren't able to establish the same empathy; there was something untrustworthy in their accents. At $199.99 per subscriber per year the stakes were too high. You had to pay an American.
The job got to him. Conning old people out of their cat food money. And of course the screaming, the cursing, the threats. God dammit you cancel this right the fuck away or I'll call the Attorney General and have your job. There were follow up calls he had to make to people who'd backed out and it was always how DARE you call me during DINNER! Well don't answer the phone then, jerkoff. But it hurt. To do the job well you had to open some part of yourself up to these people and when you were opened up they'd scream at you. Back then he was killing himself to get through those ten hours and get back home to her.

The new medications were covered by insurance. It was a pill in those days; you took it with breakfast and forty five minutes later you ceased forming new memories. He was nervous, but on the first day he came to swimming in and out of remembering in his car, and there was a post-it on the dash. He had beaten the office's all time one day record for customer retentions. On the passenger seat was a joke trophy the guys kept in the break room. You knew, when you were "under," that it all didn't matter. You were the same person but you knew it would be like it never happened. You sucked it up and you kicked ass and baby got a new pair of shoes.

He had gotten ahead. Or so they told him. He was the top retainer of customers in the division and supervised a handful of his fellows. Emily didn't have to work anymore. The cars got better and the houses got bigger. Every day he came home bright and fresh as a daisy, smiling. Emily was there with a chicken pot pie. The light of his life. She had cleaned the house and carefully rolled out a thousand layers of pastry for the chicken pot pie crust, which she layered in a becoming manner across the top. He was 44 now, although he hadn't experienced about 10 of those years.

One day, about a half hour before his shift ended, his stent broke. And he was awake.

He was on all fours. His belly was full, impossibly full, something big and hot was pushing into him and it hurt. He craned his neck around. A black man the size of a Tyrannosaur was palming his ass with a hot hand while he forced what felt like a yule log into him. The man was covered in shiny black painted-on latex and was not smiling. He himself was wearing a dress, a ballerina's dress, and there was something in his mouth. It was a ball gag coated in something like Vick's Vap-o-Rub that made his eyes water. He scrambled away on his hands and knees, screaming into the gag. It took what felt like minutes to squirm off the startled guy's member. He was in a huge room, impossibly huge, a cathedral lit by fire and all around him impossible horrible things were happening. A long dining room table with children eating from a tureen of human shit, an elderly woman skewered by a screaming stallion, everywhere dozens of people and animals were being fucked, being tortured, screaming, laughing, crying. High above at a podium Saul Krauss, of the Connecticut Krausses, Chairman and CEO of United Los Angeles Times/America Online Incorporated, was overseeing it all, issuing commands, laughing and masturbating.

He got the gag off, screamed again, got up, tried to run, but found he had a diaper around his knees. Waddled wildly until he could get if off. There looked to be a door under a rack where a naked man was wired to a car battery, shrieking. He ran for it. Great Merciful God, it was unlocked. It opened into a beige hallway with synthetic carpet and florescent lights and acoustical tile. A poster of a man climbing a mountain encouraged DETERMINATION. He ran. He wanted the way out but realized he had barely ever seen the inside of his office while he could remember. Out a window he saw cars. The parking lot. To the left. Many stairs, and then he tripped and scraped his knees on the asphalt. He tasted salt. He was weeping, and the seed of many men was smeared across his face. He puked, and ran some more. The parking space, in fucking Siberia. He sped home, gibbering and crying.

She wouldn't be expecting him for half an hour yet. He could smell the leftover chicken pot pie reheating. He ran up the stairs. He was still in the ballerina dress but he had to see her, had to tell her. They were raping people. There was no job, no company; the whole thing was just some rich guy keeping slaves so he could jerk off. We have to get out of here. Move to out to the desert. It'll be hard with no money but I can live as long as I know you love me. She was in the bathroom; the door was half open. Her hand was in the crook of her arm, turning on her medication.

Delicious Tacos
Los Angeles, 2013

Beverly Hills Plebs

Ahh...cruising down Wilshire, turning left onto
Whittier. I'm returning from another mind-numbing
errand. What am I to really expect? Every errand
is mind-numbing—bullshit simmering in this hyper-
real grid of decrepit city, mausoleums soaking in a
whorish brew. She's a well-learned woman; she's
seen a dick or two or thirty-five hundred. That's all
these mansions are: whorehouses drowning in booze
a-la-debaucherí con sodomy-de-la-(h)whiskey.

And the Master of the mansion struts in, grabs the
McCallan robed in some obscene dollar amount
north of 500; he takes it, apishly finger fucks the
cork, coaxing it out of the virgin bottle. Then,
bending some bimbo over the bar, entrapping me,
the bartender, to a front row showing of her asshole
guzzling up 3 or 4 shots worth. But not to worry.
There's no way it's her first time being fucked
up the ass with a crowd cheering her penultimate
death. At the same time, I doubt she had a guy like
me trapped 9 inches away.

The Hills of Beverly are inhabited by a bunch of
soulless cocksuckers—sex deprived scum. I'm just
a fly making rounds unnoticed, see, so I know all.
What's going on in my brain other than
1. Refill that adulterer's vodka soda, light on the ice
"pal."
2. Go home, have a drink, and write poems
contemplating my own suicide.

here—let me refill that for you.

One falsehood I hide behind out of some despicable
joy, is when attending bar at one of my employer's
zillion dollar mansions, mausoleums, penthouses,
etc., and some bimbo who swears she's not going
to succumb to the botox'd fossils swarming her
blonde, curvaceous body, her words manufacturing
an atom bomb pussy; all of whom have been
straddling a Viagra-loaded cock since drink #3.
Twenty minutes later and that chick is sucking some
botox'd fossils' wrinkly schwanz in a hot tub.

Anyway, my favorite white lie us "Help" hide
behind is the Louis XIV.

Bitches (as they're often referred to in this house)
come in asking for top fuckin' shelf booze like
they're the dead Maharaja's wife's resurrected from
her Taj Mahal tomb; like they are Hollywood's Lady
Lazarus partying with her zombie friends. I mean...
fuck off, anyone who goes to a party or backyard
social thingy, you're out of you're fucking mind if
you think you can
1. Handle it.
2. Even be allowed or offered a taste, you fucking
trashy, out-of-actressing tramp who gave up far too
young, bouncing crypt-to-crypt, dick-to-dick. It's
your truth, not mine.

Serving 14 thousand dollar liquor to some "what's-her-face" is a joke. Don't kid yourselves. It's Crown Royal. GOD! It is seriously so satisfying on a comedic level because it's so meaningless—yet in a way, omniscient. And then they 'test their taste buds,' contemplating like a wine connoisseur, puking out statements of "this is the greatest, I've ever had, and I know my cognac," or the "mmm, I'm in heaven."

But what the hell do I know? I'm just the Help, the back-up bitch boy for miscellaneous errands and time-wasting 'social' events among paper-faced people, dull and dolled up in new, re-flapped 'n' botox'd masquerade—mostly botch jobs, sucking down vodka sodas, tequila sunrises, and bubbly after bottle of bubbly; like they're royalty—or at least projecting they're members of the royalty crowd. It's all a game of who's who that ultimately causes these rich fossils to meet their demise: becoming insignificant. ("Oh no! Anything but that!")

I've been asked for dildos where I responded saying, "I'll do ya one better—I'll bring you a ball gag I discovered in the bathroom. It's cherry red, Pulp Fiction." I've seen a thing or two in my life, and this is just LA.

I've seen these greased and tanned lice bend chicks
over on all fours near the edges of pools on astro-
turf putting greens. These lice proceed to shove
dubious $100 bills along their cracks. And for what?
To then have a random midget thrown into the mix
and Eiffel Tower-dry hump the shit out of said, now
monetized, women? This is Beverly Hills, folks.
"Stuff it or don't shoot."

Who am I? I'm like Val Xavier, soon to fly up, out and
away. I'm the groovy Hermit on the Hill, overlooking
Beverly and the greater Los Angeles skyline.

SPENCER M DE GAUTHIER-STGERMAIN

HOW TO ACHIEVE LIBERATION IN POVERTY

Thankfully we are nearly there!
We are close to complete racial representation
In regard to color-shifting emojis.

Absolute difference is most visible
In the restriction of expression.
The joy of Islamic architecture
Is its absence of idolatry;
Kosher cuisine and the deli is expressed
With the complete severance
Between both milk and meat
And in the United States
We have beef jerky.

Two-State-One-State-Red-State-Blue-State
Do we really wish America upon others?
Must we all get along?
Perhaps English butlers in China
And those old men of the Occident
With living rooms and social clubs
Inspired by the style of the opium den,
And brimming with borrowed antiquity
This is perhaps the best we can hope to be.

OR WE CAN FORCE PALESTINIANS
AND ISRAELIS TO LIVE TOGETHER
So that we can watch the blood
As it does for Black boys in the South
As it has, and will for centuries.

Make it Stick

Everyone knows I haven't done anything for weeks.
Waking up
sitting on the toilet
googling "Hot girls of Instagram."
Jerking off into the toilet, missing, wiping off
strings of yellow half-Jewish jizz,
Then getting in the shower.

Back here at work
Pop plays and we overlaugh,
sip our coffee like cats.

I have found more happiness than most,
despite being ciracumcised.
Which is pretty much the only problem
I haven't been able to handle.

Pity does not sell.
It sinks.
And it stinks.
Misery loves company
but when you're asking for help,
no one wants to be around.
The best thing
is to be a depressed millionaire.

A moderate poverty
of something
is mandatory.

A good life
is nothing
but the filling up and filling down of humors, drugs,
liquids,
the pleasant belief in meaning and in piracy
feasting in direct opposition
to your fellow man.

Unhappiness is lost laziness,
when you dare to question the pirate life.

Happiness is lying
on the deck of the ship
singing I shall be released
making death a friend
and everyone else your enemy.

ALIEN POEM

"I am a sidewalk tailor with a razor
Back on the streets of Beverly Hills
Like Robespierre I have begun
A new reign of terror
I am the committee
I am the state
I am the prisoner
This is my face."
Gloria Steinem, just read this
On the Lincoln Memorial steps
Aloud to a group,
of ten hundred thousand:
To every one of the wives of King Solomon

With bayonets and halberds
I am pushing the crowd into the White House
We are lifting the president and his staff
Into the furnace of Ur.

Of the ancients, there is only death
And a million shards
Of broken ceramic.

With a satanic cabal, in the Ennis House
I remove my tuxedo and go back and forth
With a butterfly stroke in the old pool.

Toweling off, drying my body
In the cool evening
I reaffix my cummerbund
And march into the portal
Disappearing forever,
as a permanent servant.

It's just another Sunday
In the Hills of Los Feliz
Where the artists
Have constructed their palaces

hope i nevah fuhget

riddled with memories that flow
like the Neckar
I'm in Heidelberg again, sie
Schloss Schwetzingen so close
I can smell the golden skin of Venus
and her sisters (a woody allen spin-off?)
Oma walks pleasantly with me
we find a hidden mosque on the far side
of the grounds, pink and purple
in the sun's gloss.
I tell her I'd like to visit Worms
(which is less than 75km away or so)
from our cozy flat in Altenbach
nestled among the brightest of pink
and red roses
She and Uncle Horst were never very religious
so I cross the proposal off of seeing Luther's Theses.
Instead, we drink saved-for-special-occasion wine,
talk
about Mannheim in the 60s, share squares of savory
schoko-
laten—play a good game of Mensch Argere Dich
Nicht.
Oma always wins. Even when she doesn't.
She always does.

It Popped

11:40 at night seemed the right time to be overcome
with blood pulsing through my slapstick Sammy.
(that's code for my penis. (Think outside the jello
mold))
I admit…it was a strange occurrence. I had just
finished
watching an anime. Something I have done
maaaaybe once before.
Winnetka, a name that sounds completely made up,
is where my sad, restless
slam stick took me. Pent up and on the last of my
little cancers, my performance
was
lousy, built on what I really wanted, not what was
quite literally on top of me.
And then I remembered why I had stopped talking
to this—wench—mind you, I'm
working her more robust figure—and my conscience
is beckoning me to leave.
To cause shrinkage and bolt outta that clown doom.
My dna excretes from sad joystick of gloom like
cold maple syrup
a complete separation in my physiology.
Pissed off at my immature, rabbit-like need for
sexual stimulus, I fashion
a quick fib and get the hell out.

Walking a few blocks back up to my car, now
2:10am, I pine for an aristocratic assembly
to be held between my synapses, neurons, and
fertile-soft brain tissue
to discuss my idiotic behavior.
Guzzling down a road-pick-me-up set of wiiings,
a greyish cat sprints into the street
where a car is passing at roughly 65 mph.
Not having a clue what hit it, the cat quite literally
popped—like a sausage
casing—and squirmed along the median lines
awaiting death.
I jazzercise walk the rest of the way to my car,
hoping I can reach it in time to
put it out of its misery.
By the time I've turned the corner, all that remains
is a puddle of feline body juices.

I get two 7eleven mini donuts with a Nesquik,
Marlboro lites on the side.
Back at home, it's only 4:08am
and the goddamn rooster next door is
cock-a-doo-da-loo-da-ling.

Worshipping Beauty is a Horrible Mistake

A suicide net on the Golden Gate Bridge.
That's where we should stop,
save the rest.

There are building-sized dicks on billboards
hanging in cotton.
The trick is a strap around the base of the balls
and dick at once.
That way the viewer can distinguish the form of the
penis and scrotum,
which is essential to any successful campaign.

For women it's so much worse
horse liniment on the eyelids
half-lives of magazine advice
oil injected into the subderma
black hematomas
a shelf life of 10 years.

At least they're forced to become resentful of it.
Men never do.
We, fools, continue trying to be the best forever.

Beauty is not to be worshipped,
but suggested.
Perceived only from the peripheral vision
or with heavy sunglasses on
like the sun.

Lazy

This water tastes
like a rusty subway bar,
my self
sits on the edge of its couch.
It's not very comfortable.

There you go.
Now pay.

How many times
has a certain kind of person
thought about writing
"this poem sucks"
in the middle
of a poem
they're too lazy to change?

THE CHARMING WAY

"Let's be real. Feminism
Is a complete and utter waste;
It will be a matter of time
Until culturally we move past.
Why even debate it,"

Said the Chevalier de Montfoucault
To the banker M. de Kerigariou

"D'accord," it's agreed,
Said the Chevalier to me

The art of femininity is
To make a person
Pleasant, kind, and diminutive.
Such a creature is easier
To cohabitate with.

It can be defined simply:
As graceful personality,
For gentleness is the highest
Of all human behavior

Femininity is magnanimous
Giving space is generous
(What a charming way to be)

THE DEALING GAME

Once again we're at dinner
With all of the dealers
He says his wife is thirty-six
But she looks at least ten years older,
"Well then she just needs the plastic,"
I comment, "It's normal,"
"Right now she's au natural,
But it's really pretty simple."

The Pink Panthers
Break into my hotel room
At gunpoint, in the Rio Los Vegas
I've got to give up all of my product
Once again, to the Serbians.

Shysters-hucksters-wheeler-dealers
Sideshow scammers and cheaters
Abominable humanoid-scum suckers
Anyone from Florida
It's all the same

SPENCER M DE GAUTHIER-STGERMAIN

In the bar of the Delano,
There's a beautiful blonde in a little dress
She's got green eyes or blue ones
I can't help be impressed
She seems to want to get to know me
But her gaze keeps darting
To what's on my wrist

We have a few pear martinis but
The last thing I remember
Is her soft arm, interlinked with my own
And a shared glass of Dom Perignon

Waking with dried saliva crusted
In a ring around my lips
Completely naked on the floor
I try to check the time
But there is nothing there anymore.

Boredome........... ennui

It's hard to be rich
But it's so easy to be
Between these manicured gardens
I go to many museums;
Thankfully there are a lot
Of boutique restaurants for me

With transvestites
Riding in Uber
My driver
Tells me about it,
The phenomenon of driving them
And not being sure of their gender
And then I experience it
From the standpoint of a passenger
Later that evening:
He couldn't tell if she was a girl,
"It's not a huge deal," I said

We stop in front of Lure,
And let out a sleeping straight man
The drool is leaking from his maw.
As the driver taps the back of his skull
He wakens, and knows immediately
That this is just the place he wanted to be
He springs out of the car with his body

SPENCER M DE GAUTHIER-STGERMAIN

It's so easy to be bored by love
It's so easy
But then do it instead
In the dark
(The way it was intended
By the holy Universe)

"I never go to Beverly Hills," She said,
And I knew it was a lie,
Everyone makes it to Beverly Hills,
At some point in their lives
Most often for a specialist practitioner

I saw an old man on Cannon Drive
He was bleeding from the mouth
His whole lips and stubble were scarlet
And he held his red teeth in a grimace

Speaking with a forty-eight year old Frenchman
The most handsome man I have ever seen
Half-Black, Half-French, a jiu-jitsu champion
In the kitchen, surrounded by Andy Warhol
Damien Hirst, and original Cy Twomblys,
He tells me about his lesbian daughter.
It's a lot of fun being a male model
In the kitchen of a Mexican millionaire

I'M COLLECTING A CERTAIN TYPE OF FOLLOWER [REWOLLEF FO EPYT NIATREC A GNITCELLOC M'I]

Outside of a dumpster
Where the fetuses are supposed to go
Masked persons gather
With neon orange bags

A Lincoln MKX arrives
The passenger passes
A black leather briefcase
Through the open tinted window

The bag is packed tight
With orange plastic
And the car speeds off
To the aero port

This is the New El Dorado
The Transworld Elites have found the fountain
Of Juan Ponce de Leon

SPENCER M DE GAUTHIER-STGERMAIN

Upon Capitol Hill
There are countless pedophiles;
They worship the blood of youth
Through ritual human termination

Stem cell collection is the latest hobby
Of our, American senators
They're building train sets out of them

Meeting with long-brained Annunaki
In a subterranean section
Of the Belorusskaya train station
Documents are spilling
From my Swaine Adeney Brigg valise
Sweat is dripping
From my F/W 2019 PRADA flat cap

I'm just trying to get away
From CIA!

COPING WITH HER LUXURIANT FAME

Many youth approach
They come up for a common inquiry:
How do you write such fantastic poetry
It's simple, I admit
Just get to know me

Beside a Russian samovar
Boiling water for tea
I smoke a long-stemmed pipe
With a bowl of Latakia tobacco
And drink old Bordeaux from a thimble

Soothsaying
Causing the blind to see
The summoning of fire
Necromancy

(There are only so many ways
To impress the populace)

But with the air and the breath
In a garden
Or by a roadside,
It would sound like enough
And is for a while
But then you need, unfortunately
The submission of a woman

I can remember my mother's arm when I was young
And meanwhile comparing it
To the skin of her mother, who sat beside her
And to the soft skin of my own
"Your skin," I said
And she did not like it

An entrepreneur in the desert
Gin and water
All of those men who sacrificed,
Even Rudyard Kipling!
But the Brit's couldn't stick to their guns
If they had only continued with their malice
They could have taken the whole world!

And now, even I write in English
But watch it fade away
And soon, after long enough
They will no longer be able to decipher
My alien script

PRODUCT REVIEW: TENGA® EASY BEAT EGG™ ARTIFICIAL VAGINA, "SILKY"

The fucksleeve came in the mail on a Tuesday. Just like a real woman it took forever to come, he thought. There's a joke you'll never be able to tell in public.

As promised it was in discreet packaging. A surprisingly small box. Within this was a plastic egg that contained the fucksleeve. While small, it could be stretched, per the pamphlet, "to accommodate any size penis." There were also hints on how to maximize sensation on the glans and frenulum; some artist had been paid to draw a hand in various positions stretching this piece of silicon over a healthy-sized member. It's a living. Inside the thing's orifice was a single use packet of lube, but he opted for Curel Intensive Care instead. Save the special stuff for a rainy day.

I'll spare you the details. It was the first one he'd ever used and he came almost instantly, grudgingly pulling the device off of him and spraying into the sink to avoid a long cleaning process. Just like a real woman it makes you nut too fast, he thought. Just like a real woman it makes you pull out.

He'd bought the cheapest one that got good reviews. Miserly. He hadn't read the fine print, that it was so cheap and came with a packet of lube because it was intended for a single use. At the bottom of the directions pamphlet were the words "After pleasuring, discard. Try more of our 8 different textures." After about the fifth time it began to get grippy and loose, and no longer excited him. He had one last hurrah, with the single use dedicated lube packet, which made his penis smell like almonds. He emptied his seed in it, imagined he was launching an unwanted baby into fertile young loins. He then threw it out with the trash on top of some coffee grounds.

****

A few weeks later he was making chicken. He often cooked for dates, but this was a special dish he only made alone. A Vons Family Pak of 99 cents per pound chicken parts baked in Kraft barbecue sauce. His mother had always made it on his birthday, and now he would make it after a rough day at work. He would have been embarrassed if anyone saw. He liked people to think he was the type of person who seared locally caught fish with fresh rosemary. Then the doorbell rang. It was the Tenga® Easy Beat Egg™ Artificial Vagina, "Silky."

She was crying. I'm sorry, she said. I just had a really bad date, I was in the neighborhood. I had to get away from him. I'm sorry, I'm sorry, I should have called. But can I come in?

Sure, he said. He didn't know what else to say. He'd been drinking wine. He was not prepared for his artificial vagina to come to life and stop by for dinner.

Thank you. It was raining outside; she was shivering a little. What are you making? It smells wonderful.

Oh, just some, uh... just some stupid shit. Something my mom used to make.

It smells wonderful.

Thanks. It's not really, it's uh... not fancy.

Can I have some?

He blanched for a second. He had never cooked for her, obviously. Only fucked her and rinsed her off and put her back in a drawer. He would never have even considered cooking this chicken for a guest, certainly not a date. But, so what if she thought it was stupid. Who stops by someone's house unannounced. A guy who fucked you five times and threw you out. Who cared what she thought.

He served her. Then himself. She cut off a bite and blew on it. Tasted it.

Omigod... it's soooo good!

Haha. Really?

It's the best chicken I've ever had.

It's just some stupid comfort food, my mom used to make it for my birthday.

Well your mother was wonderful.

They ate and listened to the rain. She finished her plate and asked for more. Girls never did that.

Listen, she said, I know this is imposing, but can I stay here tonight? I have a movie in my bag. I'll stay out of your hair. I took the bus to my date and it's raining and I don't want to be alone.

It was out of nowhere but he didn't know how to say no. The movie was Andrei Rublev by Tarkovsky, an epic about medieval Russia. There were sweeping battles and ancient vistas and they threw a horse down a flight of stairs. It was a masterpiece. He had never talked to her about movies, obviously. He hadn't known she had such wonderful taste. They fell asleep on the couch together, her back warming his chest while the rain hissed in the leaves. In the morning she was gone.

****

A week later she called him. He didn't recognize the number but picked up anyway. Hi, she said. I don't want to be weird but I'm going to the desert this weekend and wanted to see if you'd come with me. I rented a room at this place where there's a natural hot spring.

He had been living in Los Angeles for eight years and had never seen the desert. Work had wrecked him; it was Friday night. She might be crazy but why not.

In the morning they drove out to Desert Hot Springs in her convertible. He watched the hills roll by, the plants and rocks change, and was excited. New birds circled the highway. New flowers grew in the ditch. He made her pull over so he could take a picture with a cactus.

She had a hotel room in a little place that had hot mineral water, catered to German tourists. They sat in the giant tub, naked, as dusk fell over the desert and a roadrunner came up to drink from the pool. Crickets sounded and a coyote howled. A wind blew in from the mountains and shook a wall of bamboo behind them. He was the happiest he'd ever been in his life.

They stayed together for a year. He did not remove his OKCupid profile, and he did not list himself as being "in a relationship" with his former artificial vagina on facebook. He did not introduce her to his friends. But she came over three nights a week, or during the day when her air conditioning broke, and they laid around watching movies and drinking wine and talking. They camped in the mountains, cataloging the national forest's twenty four different kinds of rodents. They didn't fuck anymore. He cared about her too much. You have to want to hurt somebody to fuck them. They tried a few times and he would look in her eyes and it would make him laugh.

****

In the spring she had a doctor's appointment. She called him after, crying. Said she needed to come over. She had cancer, she said. There were going to be treatments but she probably wasn't going to make it. We are going to beat this, he said. You are going to beat this. No, I'm not, and I need you to do something for me. She had no one. No family. If I get to the point where I might live but wouldn't be me anymore, she said, I need you to have them pull the plug. He didn't know how he would ever do it, but, how could he say no.

He would drive her to chemo, to radiation; she would tell him stories in the car. About her childhood. Things she'd never told anybody but had to tell someone now, otherwise it would be like they never happened. She had been through a lot, it turned out. Men passing her around since she was a baby. The life of a fucksleeve. The radiation burned her skin and the drugs made her throw up all the time and she started slipping away. He would sit with her under the IV bag and hold her hand. She was slipping but she was still her; she could still make him laugh.

The drugs didn't work and she needed surgery. He was in the waiting room reading the hospital's copy of Reptile magazine, for domestic reptile enthusiasts. The featured review was of the Tomato Frog. They may look drab when young, but don't be fooled: they explode into a vivid red-orange in adulthood. Especially the somewhat larger female. An engaging and active amphibian. He wondered what it would take for Reptile to give a bad review. He moved on to The Hunt for the Dark Phase Everglades Corn Snake and noticed his hands were shaking.

A doctor came out. There had been a complication. One of the tumors was near an artery and they had nicked it. She was on blood thinners and was bleeding out. She might never wake up. If she did, her brain had been deprived of oxygen. She would not be herself. I understand that her wish was not to be resuscitated. We have some papers you'll need to sign. They let him hold her hand while she died, with that stupid machine beeping like on TV.

She had been sick for a long time, skinny and gray with sunken eyes and no eyebrows and most days she could barely talk. But that wasn't how he remembered her, driving home and trying not to break down and cry in traffic. He remembered the desert. The hot spring. Kissing her in the warm water, the wind whipping the bamboo back and forth. It would hurt him forever, the way she left him, but he wouldn't trade it for the world.

In conclusion: five stars.

Delicious Tacos
Los Angeles, 2013

idol idyllic.

So many speak about Jack Kerouac
but hardly do anything

Don't get me wrong; for a great deal of time,
I grew up
on asthmatic mentholatum spreads
and various styles
of church pew.
Some traditional oak or cedar, others with
cup holders—more movie theater—with pastors &
preachers,
ministers & teachers, scholars et al doctors
on VHS tape, counting the meta_____physical
hours
of moments saying,

"this" "is"   "way"
    "the" "to"   "the" "_____."
        "to"
            "the"
                "_____."

TIMOTHY BARNETT

Don't tell me.
I get it.

If all roads lead to said Roman Rx
none and all are
potential salvations
potential loveships to sink
and sail.
potential idols to salivated
and covet,
part of that mirage-core music scene
idyllic.

We are the sword as much
as we are the sheath.

Like a horse before the cart
How you push is how she_____starts.

SPENCER M DE GAUTHIER-STGERMAIN

ONCE UPON A TIME IN THE BACK ALLEYS OF RODEO DRIVE

The back alleys of Rodeo Drive
Smell worse
Than those of any others
In the country
Save for maybe, Madison Avenue

Here there's a lot that's rotten
A carpet of scum
A fifty-inch crystal wine decanter
In the Beverly Wilshire

Inside the Peppermint Club
Everyone is Drake or Kanye
But mostly a girl from a Weeknd music video
Or an agent on a date
Everyone might be having a good time?
We're in the Peppermint Club
Sniffing juice

In the bars of Beverly Hills
Sniffing that record player juice
Now I'm in a 1920s jazz cartoon!
For exactly two minutes,
Walking down the street
With every step--
My knees trigger up beyond my pelvis
And my hands alternate
Behind my back and above my shoulders.
When it fades, just another respiration
Takes us back to Tex Avery

SPENCER M DE GAUTHIER-STGERMAIN

[I'm a snake in the Beverly Hills grass]

But you gotta believe me on this
The foreign girls love sniffing the bottle
It really opens you up,
That record-cleaner juice
The tumblers of Japanese whiskey
Continue rolling in

Smoking Abu-Hamza medwakh
From a marble dokha
We hide our pipes in our packs
And drink Macallan on the rooftop
With the princes of Saudi Arabia
By the pool of the Hotel Sixty

Though harems await our friends,
We traveling European men,
Can only hope
For abduction from their seraglio

Blondes in white Mercedes whip past me
Dipping into underground parking
A few minutes later with a dog
And yoga outerwear

Those born to wealth
Are formed with infantile souls
They are new to existence

SPENCER M DE GAUTHIER-STGERMAIN

A mental mistake
Is often made,
Culture has no ends
It is as a continuum

I have burrowed here
In my rabbit nest, but
Beverly Hills is a den of snakes, truly!
At the base of the Hills of Bel-Air
The land particularly,
Teems and froths with them there.

I am Hercules marching over
The Hills of Beverly
Wandering and searching
With my nephew Iolaus.
There are serpents here,
There are gorgons there
I see them walking with their terriers
Taking in the evening air
They have nice clothes and blond hair
But of the men, doubly beware!

CULPABILITY POEM

Ernest Hemingway
Told the truth, anyway:

"Don't be fooled friends,
Our culture LOVES pussy
But pulling away at our highest moment
Of divine ecstasy,
By Epicurean philosophy,
Has been ingrained in us:
A society that is afraid of the uterus
Does not love women.
We were born to end there."

POPULATE POPULATE THE EARTH
BIRTH THE GENIUSES
OF THE NEXT GENERATION
BABIES WILL LEAD TO EQUALITY:
EVENTUALLY, ARMIES WILL BE UNABLE
TO BE FORMED LARGE ENOUGH
TO ADEQUATELY POLICE URBANITY

This is the fear
It is why Bill Gates loves contraception

The globalists and cold-blooded lizard overlords
Wish for your death!
At the end of productive life
Without any children

ISAAC SIMPSON

Truth Will Get You

When your son comes to you really suffering

You don't say you look very handsome today
You don't say there's sex hormones in your water
You don't say I'm feeling bullish
about Taiwan Semiconductor (TSMC)

When your sister comes to you
at the very bottom of her life

You don't say lose a few pounds
You don't say humans share 98% of their DNA
with bullfrogs
You don't say jet fuel doesn't melt steel beams

When your best friend loses everything

You don't say they found water on the moon
you don't say hot Yoga opens the pores
of the mind and body
you don't say Bruce Willis was dead the whole time

What you do say is the one thing in the entire world

that you know

is not true.

Singing Psalms of Praise to Jean Paul Marat and Alex Jones

I am transformed from nothing
Into opinions
Into a person

I have intense knowledge of taste
Which is the illusion of character

The secret of life
Is that everyone around
Is Live Action Role-Playing

The beliefs of the greater part of humanity
Are arbitrary completely
One hundred years ago
In western society
Women's ankles you could not see;
But in two hundred CE
Flagellation was public spectacle

SPENCER M DE GAUTHIER-STGERMAIN

It's fun to ski down a glacier
It's fun to be a shark hunter
It's fun to buy contemporary art

Surrounded by white women
With slim figures
Big lips and small noses
Sunglasses and freckles

In Harry Cipriani in Brickell Miami
Somewhere after the fourth
And before sixth Bellini
Switching between e-cigarettes
And real cigarettes
Depending upon with whom I am speaking
There is a nervous energy
But everybody knows me

Peck Rd South

and just like that the Bigger Bird landed and they were gone
in a southbound trajectory, fueled like Christians
who claim to witness a miracle
Painting the sky a sheet of black,
all on a beautiful chill day.

x x x

And then, about 45 minutes later,
I spot these birds, possibly jacked, possibly
vanishing from a rough nest, sitting.
Sitting above the 10 fwy at Peck Rd South.

ISAAC SIMPSON

Mellors

I did San Pedro with six men in their thirties.
One rang a sound bowl.
One puked fluids and words.
One ate more drugs.
One spread love.
One hoarded water.

I squashed the fire-blanched bushes.
Felt brittle bones snapping under my boots.
I ripped baby plants out of the earth
and put them on display.
I held meat over flames
dipped it in the sand
and swallowed it.
I knocked branches off seaweed trees
and loved to watch them melt.
I climbed boulders to stop the moving sky
and I looked over the other men.
I poured whiskey on my hands
to heal 1,000 cactus needle cuts.

I didn't feel oneness or love.
I felt fear and craving.
To digest the desert
to eat the sand.
To boil the blue-green former sea plants into mescal
and let it run into my pores.
To learn every angle of the sticks and buds,
and crush them into a tasty salt.

What's My Tribe?

Today, in The New Yorker,
a great cushioned bohemian
admitted that he's a tribalist.
He tried everything
before settling on Judaism
The hero returning home
after a long journey
funded by his parents.

If it were today
there would be photos of the girl he was fucking
at a particular point in his soul searching.
She would be drinking a glass of Retsina
with sunglasses covering her face.

Kosher bakeries on Pico
with signs made of molded plastic
.37 pounds per letter
the inch of dust on each maybe brings it up to .40.
Inbred believers in black,
headfeathers of velvet and wool,
Shtreimel and the chanting of crows.
Culture as thick
as the paint on the walls
of an old Manhattan apartment
each chip a rainbow of time.

ISAAC SIMPSON

The bohemian
took acid
on stage
in Jerusalem
he said that the crowd turned into one single Jew.

Then there's my black friend Travis
We drove through a lesbian neighborhood
in Chicago
on a warm November evening.
The molded rubber drooping out
of the window socket
of his decrepit Mitsubishi.

I remembered his grandmother
Handing me a small brown plate
with a piece of sweet potato pie on it.
His uncle grilling a hot sausage with red grease
and saying to me,
"Don't worry. We've got mild too."

Then there's Tim who's just white
but has decided to be Swedish.
And Sally who's prairie white
but studied Jewish studies
And a lot of Jewish cocks
while she was at it.

And then there's all the men
pretending to be women
And all the women
pretending to be slaves.

I think what we want
more than anything
is to be rolled over.
That's how you get a culture
thick like paint
in an old Manhattan apartment.

OH EVERYONE'S DOING RUBBINGS NOW

It's easy to rub your own poem down
Rub rub rub
Rub-a-dub
My dirty body in the filthy tub
Robespierre Roger Herman Rod Serling
Rub-a-dub
Three musketeers in a tub

Take any textured surface
And make a poem of it:
Tree bark poem
Carpet poem
Gravestone poem

Rub your poem onto me
Rub my poem onto you
It's just easy to do

SPENCER M DE GAUTHIER-STGERMAIN

BUT WERE THERE EVER ANY TOWERS

It's so easy when you're driving
To crash the car, melting to infinity
It's so easy to drive it's so easy
For your particles to be disbursed
Throughout the nether regions of the universe

Sixty five thousand hotdogs
Ordered, in the John Podesta emails
For Barack Obama
Seven boys of different sizes
And in different colors
In a hot tub
They'll be happy, trust me

Karl Lagerfeld in his nightgown
Drinking Diet Pepsi
Drawing bare boys
In under three wrist-strokes

Humans are sun-based life forms
Full of radioactivity!
They are but short lived;
Burning up from cancer
Killed like bees

But the intergalactic messengers,
Our inter-dimensional angels
Are interacting with the chosen:
Those possessors of billions,
They're trying to put an end
To human cognitive evolution(!)

SPENCER M DE GAUTHIER-STGERMAIN

A hand pushes down
For us to remain in the dust
Of the third dimension

I am a dinosaur

In the moment when
It is realized
That human speech
Is only the flapping
Of meaty membranes
In measured order
Against tongue and teeth:
You're trying to sell a Rolex

Bark bark bark
My octopus tentacle flails
And in mediation
Says what it believes
In the parlor room
Beside the kitchen

Stray Cat On The Bar-B-Que, Staring At A Hummingbird Hum Over Molding, Orange, Crustaceous Blossoms

Drugs are in part culprit to the weight carried on
our shoulders.
At least mine, right?
That's why we're here, right? Give something to get
something?
We're either scared as hell to even be around them,
let alone be up close
in person to them, or we're
balls to the balls dgaf to try them; usually "hit it."
You become
the cool kid, the music deadbeat,
the washout (pretty much
the identical twin brother to the music deadbeat),
the artsy-moody poet type the know-it-all classicalist
(pretty much the *paternal twin sister to the artsy-
moody poet types. The difference is
that one wears Hot Topic for a while then becomes a
normal
struggling artist while the other wears American
Eagle/Hollister for a while
then gets knocked up by the jock or businessman
crass politician type, locking herself in the closet
semi-annually
to contemplate suicide from her cookbook of death—
dreaming, always dreaming, why she gave it all up
and how it would have been better

to explore lesbianism and
grow out her armpit and leg hair—maybe the upper lip, go by
"Pat" instead of Patricia for a minute," really hit the female genitalia and her divine
priestess... maybe live in SF with a college student a few years her
junior, going to powerful liberal marches and protests against crooked ex-
husband's (or those who very well could have been.). At least that's part of
what I saw growing up in The Mojave. Only part. Drugs are pretty scary the first time (but
secretly sooo badass). They're illegal—later
becoming more so legal—so they carry that unknown stigma.
"Does it really
help them?" "Is my baby a *lost lamb of god?" "Oh, they're
idiots wasting they're money and playing with the law." In a way, that's all a little true—
since apparently there's a little truth in
every lie. Part of that delicious oyster we swallow. Guess what? Drugs ruined an entire 365 days of my life. Either I
wanted them or I had them, using and using and

using and using, really believing it was helping me,
when in reality, when you multiply $70 x 4
you get: a number. A big one, in dollars.
Sense? Pfft; out the fuckin' window.
When you're at the counter, you're going through with the buy
regardless what your ninny angel or emo demon
on your shoulders whisperwhisperwhisper. You
can't be helped. I can't be helped. Are you even listening; hello?
And then life gets poorer, can't pay the insurance, the girlfriend's been
gone, baby—way gone. Already bonin'
some other idiot because you couldn't cope with the fact that you were still broke and
living near home, loathing sheer existence. And then, you take a job, make the
"big" bucks, yet, still can't seem to pay the debts off. Why?
Because the drugzzzz have put you in a snooze.
A stall. A wait, O, God, a wait.
And even in The Still you can't seem to find it—The Still.
And you're fucking in it. Before,
this would have been God's voice kissing your

mind, but
that part of your open mind has been filled by other
bullshit. Bullshit you can't live
up to because you're stuck in a job you can't get
out of for some fucking reason and you
want to die and ram your car into oncoming traffic
but don't because you
drop your cigarette and smell a rotten trash of a fire
brewing beneath your
stupid feet in your goddamn piece of shit miracle
car.
But this is your life. My life. Our life. Sometimes.
Our
existence. Sometimes. It's all around
us. We're just fucked up
animals that can't handle the whip on our tails. Am
I talking to myself? Hello?
Hello? Hello? Hello?

HELLO?

Oil

So
I've forgotten how to write
how to bathe
how to change my crazy socks
how to clean these trousers.
They're veeeeeeeeeeery dirty.
I'm a cesspool.
Nej, I haven't forgotten how to do it
I just...it hurts and something isn't working
the way it used to.
The music of the words. Their timbre.
The way words can tear open your fucking heart
and then sew it back together again.
I miss the way characters and their voices
would visit for coffee. That and the sound of their
songs.
A vagabond stooge, a drifter
on my desert highway, walking past the last of the
American
Indian & Cowboy shootouts. Bones and tomahawks

buried to sleep in gun powder.
Remnants of a dry lake bed.
I've lived in 10 different homes in 10 different cities
in the past year 1/2.
I bet you anything, you haven't.
Very cheap rent—that I still cannot afford. Not since
the summer.
Living each month to the penny.
Some habits are hard to break.
But I'm an addict and can't seem to shake it.
(Torso quivering, fingers frozen, feet dancing like...
...like Liberace Frenching Death.)
Honest to God though,
what ocean
am I sailing?
I've been floating and floating and floating
and even through my "music"
I haven't reached her.

Untitled Poem

Here is a sign, here is a word:
The ear of a crow

The shape of a bacterium

Peel away the skin of the world
The peel covers the fruit

Now we can begin to see
Behind the skin
Behind the feather of the crow
Fake news
The coin slot ear of the crow:
Look now!
Peer into the infinite chasm

SPENCER M DE GAUTHIER-STGERMAIN

The world is empty of blood
Mankind has no intention
The world is empty of blood

The rich have inherited the earth

How little and dark is the human window
Gazing upon the Hanging Gardens
I am here where there is only desire
For fame and wealth
Surrounded by the heavens
Just across from the stones
Of the ruined tower of Nebuchadnezzar
I pause a moment reflecting
Prince of princes,
Upon the high ziggurat

SHIT JOBS: MCDONALD'S

I was sixteen and my mom made me get a job. Again. Learn the value of work. She was right, it's a lesson I retain decades later: the value of work is less than fucking zero, a negative eating away at your soul and your life. So, thanks. I applied at the McDonald's in Kingston, Mass.

You had to buy your own McDonald's shirt and special synthetic pocketless pants so you couldn't walk out with a ninety nine cent hamburger warmed to ass temperature. They took the money out of your first couple checks. The checks came three weeks late; they'd docked sixty eight bucks for the uniforms they'd sold you, and taxes were taken out, something like a third of your check. At that point you'd been working dozens of hours in the sweltering hissing clamoring kitchen, alarms constantly blaring, six hundred degree grills an inch away from the meat of your hands, swabbing the greasy tiles over and over with a filthy mop every time there was a two second lull in orders, getting yelled at– you got your check and it was fucking nothing. You had known what taxes were in an abstract sense, the ten per cent federal tax bracket, but what you didn't know was state tax, city tax, FICA, SDI... weird acronyms... your check came an ungodly amount of time later and there was nothing left. The value of work. Cleaning the toilet, a filthy log of shit breaching in piss yellow water with toilet paper snaked over the bowl and onto the floor about one out of every four times you went in there–the value of work.

Girls were up front and boys were in the back. In theory it was an equal opportunity workplace free of gender discrimination but not a single girl worked the spattering grill or dollied sixty pound cases of frozen beef patties down to the dark freezer or hauled trash bags the size of refrigerators full of imperfect meat out to the dumpster. Not a single guy ran the cash register or talked to customers. People want to see a smiling girl with perky tits. I don't blame them. The girls worked up front and didn't flirt with us or really talk to us at all. They were the house slaves. They had to take the heat when we fucked something up; they were the ones getting scolded that "I told you no onions." They must have seen us as fuckups and miscreants.

My job was the Quarter Pounder With Cheese and McLean grill. It is an excellent station, if you ever work at a McDonald's. The volume is significantly lower than hamburger/ cheeseburger/ Big Mac and you're not dealing with a big deep pit of face-melting frying oil. Plus, the Quarter Pounder was my preferred sandwich as a civilian. When people ordered what I made, I mentally congratulated them for making the correct choice. The hamburger is a trifle, not really food at all; you polish it off in two bites and feel like you've eaten greasy air. The Quarter Pounder is a real sandwich. A connoisseur's sandwich.

You take the patties from the freezer to the left of your grill and drop them on the griddle surface frozen. They hiss and steam. There's a clamshell lid with another heated surface that you lower on top of them, and the meat is done in ninety seconds. The clamshell grill is a proprietary McDonald's technology that a training video has explained to you preserves maximum freshness and sanitation in the meat. A light flashes and a distinctive bell sounds and you lift the clamshell lid and spatula the burgers onto the buns you've prepared. You have caramelized the buns in a toasting unit which has its own distinctive lights and a buzzer that you will hear in your dreams. A training video has explained that you caramelize the buns to prevent them from absorbing the condiments and becoming soggy. I liked that they didn't condescend to you– they kept the word "caramelize" instead of some proprietary corporate buzzword that was less hard to say. Caramelize. Ketchup, mustard out of big metal cups with handles where you pull a trigger and it dispenses the perfect amount; pickles laid with care not to overlap, onions. You drape two slices of cheese offset at a forty five degree angle so there is cheese in every bite. The videos are good at explaining why you do things. They didn't need to; they could have just told me put the cheese at a forty five degree angle because I fucking said so, but they took the time and I appreciated it. Wrap the sandwich in the snug origami-like proprietary McDonald's fashion. Quarters up.

You get a rhythm. Lunch rush comes and you are anticipating the buzzes and beeps and chimes and lights; you are ahead of the game and the heat lamp rack is not wanting for fresh Quarter Pounders for even one second. No shrill "WHERE ARE MY QUARTERS??!?" from the cashier girl and no quick huddles from the manager on how you have to up your game. I can't have guys keeping us behind on this team, OK? "Grill orders," which is the bespoke no onions type of stuff– most grill crew hated those. I loved them. You knew you were preparing a sandwich for one particular person just the way they liked it. A machine spat out instructions on receipt tape in purple ink and you had to run over and grab them and hustle to make the sandwich. When you fucked one up the manager would walk back with the tape and point out to you what it said and ask you: how did this happen? You forget that it's McDonald's; it's literally the least prestigious job in the world, people laugh at you for having it, and your net income is two dollars and fifty cents an hour. You are terrified and you feel bad about yourself. The value of work.

You get a rhythm, and it gets fucked up by having to restock the patties, go to the back and get more buns, empty and sanitize the ketchup dispensers. If things slow down at all the manager will constantly bark at you for a sweep and mop. Wrestle with the filthy greasy mop in the sink and maybe cut your hands on some industrial tomato slicing device soaking there. Not one second is wasted; you are a perfect machine working constantly. McDonald's is the best managed company in the world, right down to the slightly subnormal woman with a weird limp who smokes unfiltered Pall Malls who's in charge of your shift– she has been indoctrinated perfectly in how to make your day tight as a drum. You aren't grilling, you take out the trash, you sweep and mop. Drill sergeants aren't this good. Her name was Wendy but she insisted on being called "Romayne."

We would fuck with her. She hated being called "Wendy" so when she turned her back we would start singing "Wendy" over and over. Me and Glenn, a kid from Marshfield who ran McNuggets and french fries. Glenn was funny and smart. I was funny and smart too, and it was the first of many shit jobs where I'd find another funny and smart person and we'd kind of marvel at "what the fuck are you doing here."

I'd be bummed out when I showed up for a shift and Glenn wasn't there. We had an imaginary ranking system for all the cooks– you start out as a Grill Knave, moved up to Grill Apprentice, Grill Soldier, Grill Master, Grill Wizard, Grill Lord. The highest level was Grill God. Only one man had ever achieved it and he'd ascended into the Golden Arches and become a hamburger himself. You now know him as Mayor McCheese. We had long running stories about defending our McDonald's from the conspiracies of the Burger King, Big Dave Thomas, and Colonel Sanders.

We'd get a really good riff going and then "Romayne" would come yell at us for a sweep and mop. Not one second wasted. They will get as much out of you as possible for as little as possible, and rightly view human interaction between employees as wasteful. This is good management. Some companies call this "time theft," talking to the people you work with. They own time. They own your life, and you are stealing it. The value of work.

I took a week off because I was in the school play. When I came back they had completely gutted the store and reorganized all the machines. A new process had been instated by corporate for each food item, to insure that every McDonald's meal was even hotter and fresher than before. They had installed something called a "Q'ing oven." The "Q" stood for "quality." If a customer asked what it was, you were to say "it's just something we do to make your food taste better."

The Q'ing oven was a microwave. But you were NEVER to refer to it as a microwave. In fact, they said, from now on, you are NEVER to use the word "microwave" while inside the store. Whether you are at the register, at the grill, or in the break room. Whether your shift has begun or not. If you are heard using the word "microwave," you will be fired immediately and escorted from the building.

It was the "big" manager who gave this talk, Mark. The one who went to Hamburger University. The degree was framed in his office where there was a mop bucket and an ancient Tandy PC he would use to enter our hours to the second. That's how you knew it was some serious shit– him talking to us was like a presidential address. And the word was so doubleplus ungood that Mark seemed scared of saying "microwave" even in the sentence "you must never say the word 'microwave.'"

Mark wasn't a bad guy, although I never forgave him for the time I fried my hand on the clamshell grill and got a blister from my pinky to my elbow, and he just scotch taped a bandage on it and made me work the rest of my shift. But he was human. He was just beaten down from fear of losing his job at McDonald's, fear of bringing nothing home to his family. He just got so indoctrinated with corporate bullshit that he had to spend his days making a room full of teenagers terrified of saying "microwave." The value of fucking work.

I left, but not before earning a ten cent raise as a "senior grill crew" member and a special pin for how long I'd worked there and how little I'd fucked up. Every job I've ever had since has been exactly the same. Someone clogged the toilet and some asshole is yelling at you to fix it, and you'll get fired for saying what shit really is.

Epilogue:

I checked them out on Yelp. See how the alma mater's doing. They have one star. "Order had errors. Fries were not warm. Sauce pumps were all empty. My meal came with a drink and I had to remind them. Counter was dirty. My filet only had half a piece of cheese and no extra tarter sauce like I asked."

Fuckin Grill Knaves.

Delicious Tacos
Los Angeles, 2013

Traveling

When you are from a little bit of money in America,
and if you don't do anything rash,
you will have a spot waiting for you
in a job that is not a job,
but a holding pen.
A mausoleum for your soul,
and a parking place for your will.

The job will have a three-word title
and the work will be to add your weight
to the inertia of mediocrity and repetition.
You will lament this role,
and you will say, whenever you can, that you just
don't fit in in this corporatized world,
because you are a wild stallion cowboy.

Your real job will occur on weekends
buying products and traveling.
Three weekends a month you simply must travel.
Bachelor parties and weddings,
the rest holidays, bar and bat mitzvahs, funerals,
sporting trips, and festivals of sloth and hedonism
each one of ever increasing sincerity
in its mission to be authentic.

The travel will keep you from ever having
to get to know your partner
or to get to know your home
or your neighbors
or to develop feelings of ownership over anything
besides your social media accounts.

At some point you will understand
that these flashes of identity
are your real job.
And that will make you feel safe
because someone who has been photographed
drinking a cup of coffee
glamping on Big Sur
clinking glasses
rich person
cannot be a failure who has wasted their life.

But since you are a rebel
you will recognize it
and post about it
and maybe write poems about it.

***

History is for the guillotine and the guillotine alone.
Justice is working.
Ask anyone.

Crumtples

Enjoy the film
on your soup
the engineered flavor
dust on your nuts
the feel of the heat
resistant cardboard
on your coffee cup.

Really take a moment
to run your fingers
over the leather
nook of your steering wheel
The glasses indent
on the bridge
of your girlfriend's nose.

Really feel
the brass button
on your jeans
as you run it under your fingernail.
Or the plastic pen top
in your teeth
as you chew it into crumples.

The useless click
of the elevator close button
the slight bend
in your plastic toothbrush.
The internal thump
of the gas cap
as it spins closed.

TIMOTHY BARNETT

and of course

that's why you have the job.
there'll definitely be times murder is the only way
to stop the voices cackling cackling cackling
| after work |
| over margaritas |
| spouse-free |

you'll feel racist too, because there's one
plate of food left on the tray
and the only person without sustenance
is a young black guy
right beside you in a bar booth
and oh, it just so happens that this particular dish
are "The Ape" Tacos

you'll try desperately not to laugh, as I did in this time warped
blip, at the absurdly coincidental, robotic racism.

the answer is yes.
even for a piece of garbage
job, a small part of ass
was kissed on my behalf...
and is
as
to not
(yet) get
fired.

a sweet day that will be.

Mary

By now you are pop singer
"came up playin' keys"
something to appeal to the folk crowd
it is false.

I cook my pasta
and we talk about it.
You never seemed like a Leo before,
but you do now.

By now you are in Italian vogue,
but the photographer
had to carefully
hide your thighs
under a piano.

You lived in Iowa with a boyfriend,
but something happened.
Not with the chickens.

So by now you are the kind of LA girl
who steals parking spaces
clinging to a face
that lets you do it.

Your eyes haven't gotten any
less green after all,
and your lips
are still on your face.

aluminum horse

homeless on the street
all he wants is to sleep
the bugs be gone.

so he sits in sleeping bag shoes
looking a garbáge mermaid
grocery bags his pearl revolve.

in one hand, fire awakens
the advertisement thump, his
hollywood-sunset home
while the other holds the aluminum
horse
the goop that smack across the cock
against the brain.

red light presses, car slows to a stop.
cigarette stuck dry between
my lips, tooth decay vapors percolating
through the cracked window.

I turn the radio down some.
don't want to harsh homeless man's
sleepy time ritual, ordained holy by
the priestess herself, down at the
skeeze-infested 7th Veil; that's only a couple
blocks from here.

she's always only a few blocks away
from his fire, from
his horse, for he is a victim-fallen-product
to the interworkings behind
the purple curtain.

Death by Goodness

The suicider
would be free
to bask in it
if it was just meaninglessness
but it can't be that
because the suicider isn't free
because he doesn't really believe
the meaninglessness
he thinks he does.

To get outside one's head
that's the trick
that's the drink
if only alcohol weren't so effective
"if only alcohol weren't so effective"
if only you didn't have to say if only
if only there wasn't pressure
to be good
a good boy.

Fred, the Poem

Fred is holding my champagne. It's eight pm in Los Angeles and I have decided to only ever use a typewriter. 27 FEB 2015 we're all here smoking drinking etc…and it feels like the whole world is all right.

From where it was whence it returns. Ben is talking about Uber surcharges. I'm totally uselessly drunk. And high on a little bit of cocaine that I found in the top drawer. Horseradish on my tongue.

And that's what it takes. Three shots of Knob Creek, the last only goes down half way before coming up. What is it about drinking that feels like work being done. The same with typing on this paper. Maybe in the future, there will be digital drinking, just like digital typing. Something to do with your online persona.

Typing these keys has to be the most satisfying feeling on Earth. What is it about these hammering metal sticks? Making the world letter by letter, putting your own house in, building your own thing, letter by letter, hammer by hammer, on this endless piece of paper. That's what we're doing.

Just turn away. Just turn the channel, is what people say.

There is silence now.

Then a unicorn flew into the room blunt in hand, ready for an action packed adventure. Catfish are embarrassed by you, you fool. Remember our previous discussion? Yeah, figured you didn't.

Anti-Love Poem

Our love doesn't flow like water.
It doesn't rise like a spring.
It doesn't light up the dark.
It doesn't make bluebirds sing.

Our love doesn't cross the ocean
or climb up a majestic mountain.
It doesn't make the body shake
or draw enough tears to fill a fountain.

Our love is not our love
because it's really not a noun.
Our love is not a secret whisper
passed around our town.

Our love is not an adjective
to describe our Thursday evenings.
Our love is not a parting line,
in a letter full of feelings.

ISAAC SIMPSON

Our love is not a feeling
that I haven't had before.
It's not the sun on an empty beach
or a cabin's open door.

What our love is is not a poem
but a reaction in a dish.
A scientist looks down on us
a pair of squirming fish.

But unlike fish we're not separate
but tied from fin to fin.
When I move my arm it moves yours too
and through the dish we swim.

So worry in worry out
there's no need to check the time.
We're stuck together until the end
sharing this same long spine.

LSD POEM

Death is not a Horseman
Death is a Vanity

WELCOME! To acid

Gertrude Stein
Just loved men in a different way
In a different time, she loved Ernest Hemingway
But women she loved in still another

Salamanca Spain is beautiful

WHOOPS IM BUGS BUNNY!!
AND I JUST TOOK A TAB OF LSD

red door green door
red wine good time

a cat with a craniotomy
is still curious

just like me!
his upper faculties
are just searching for something

something ancient and unknowable
THIS is the root of consciousness:
A thing which tells us only what to ignore

the books are on sale

and the tulips are dead and a young man wears a
Charlie Sheen t-shirt thinking he's a boss and he
has on shower shoes and there's a fat Chinese girl
holding phone 1/2 an inch from her uvula and she
mumbles and her belly jiggles as she walks and
I am a dweeb for thinking this and the air smells
like soup or Marie Callendar's pot pie not pot pie
French Onion soup and the air smells like garlic
salt powder and the tulips are dead and people
have forgotten how to walk and earbuds are the
new Beethoven Lennon McCartney bliss and the air
smells like soup and the tulips are dead and a girl
hides her face in blush like a turtle and girls put on
"not" and scale the rooftops and the tulips are dead
and people are staring only at the ground and not
looking at the Sun or the clouds or the breezeway
leaves on the trees and my breath smells like coffee
and my back is sweaty and it's the jean on jean
and my mood is foul and my hands smell like old
books and people in class don't shut the hell up
and I wish they'd shut the hell up and they sit back
from the chalkboard thinking they know it all and

my feet are snug in brown shoes and mix- matched
socks and I'm seriously becoming fragile like glass
that persons won't SHUT THE
HELL UP! and the air smells like kettle corn and
my hands smell like old books and my best friend
is leaving for South America for Five months and
the Family celebrated God Jul (= Christmas) and
we wear Mormor's socks made out of love and knit
wool and seriously is no one bothered by the soup-
smelling air (= ?) and I'm calming down and my
heart is beating and I want bottomless mimosas
and gins w/ tonic w/ lime maybe two and I want
her, by now we all know who she is and she is the
goddamn book and I'm needing a nap and the tulips
are dead and the tulips are dead and the tulips are
dead and the tulips are dead and the tulips are
dead and the tulips are dead and the tulips are dead
and the tulips are dead and the tulips are dead
and the tulips are dead and the tulips are dead and
the tulips are dead and the tulips are dead and the
tulips are dead and the books are on sale.

TIMOTHY BARNETT

On How to be an Angel (with Wings)

Discovering
the ways
of Love
with Scotch
Tape
is a must.

Greeting
the bottom
of the
bottle is
also a must
as right/wrong
is challenging
when dry.

Thanks to cops
scattered around
the streets
with green
gutters...

Purchase a mirror
(not necessarily
vintage like one
found in Rosebud's
Castle).
Stare at it.
Long. Hard.

TIMOTHY BARNETT

Pick up an
Instrument
and play.
One way or
another.
Even if it
feels like
a jungle.

Grimace as the
needle kisses
the grain
of the ephemeral
conversation starter
in black &
multicolored vinyl.

Dullness is a
common cork,
so find the bottom
of the shrinking
town's bottle.

SPENCER M DE GAUTHIER-STGERMAIN

DEATH DEATH DEATH DEATH DEATH DEATH DEATH

The rich are unilaterally scum

Meanwhile I find the hair of une vieille maitresse
Woven between the teeth
Of a zipper fly, in my closet
Later I find an heiress
Among my old soiled laundry –
M. Honore de Balzac would be,
With reservation, very proud of me

Ohhhhhhhhhhhh
Noooooooooooooooooooooooooo!!!
With a CRASH, they've just KILLED ME!
With a remote control
They've hijacked my Uber
At one-hundred-and-thirty
Miles of an hour, through the windshield
They've just hurled me!
(The driver survived, with minor injury)
And just as was Bob Simon,
I, another member of the Fourth Estate, Today,
vehicularly butchered;
Amidst the shattered glass
And the asphalt of the pavement
In the road I lie on my side
With my gross brown intestines
All outsplayed on the street ☺

But having come from the gutter,
I sure did bang a lot of rich girls!
How many points will that get me??

SPELL SCROLL: PENGUIN PUBLISHING WILL LOVE IT!

Half of every dollar I have made
Has gone into drone weaponry

You are still finding yourself, they say:
No I am only death incarnate
In human flesh
Nothing can be found of me

I am only blood
Beneath my skin
A single bag of red
With a pocket knife

There is a spider in my grapes
It is crushed amongst the green mass

Darkness, blankets, curtains, and cushions
Fall over me
The web of night, glittering star beams
Wash over my midnight harem

There is a spider crushed amidst my produce
I ask my handmaidens:
How many legs have I eaten?

THE HEART OF DARKNESS IS THE PLACE OF PERFECT PEACE

How do you give and how do you take
That is the action of life

Time is the expression of masculinity
Which is everything in-between;
The lobster and the human man
A central nervous system
And a dominance hierarchy

Gabriel Ananda

The fear of death and the fear of not death

No one should be trusted to it; but here we are

Surrender control in expression:

Taking photos up to the point
That the memory is full
And on the freeway
There is only death in every second

SPENCER M DE GAUTHIER-STGERMAIN

And again, the sacrifice:
Everything is between the pulsating moments
Between unbeing and being

The Eye of Horus and the Eye of Ra
Reverberation of the beach
In the morning
Is paralleled in the exhalation
And inhalation of the moist clouds at dawn
We view it all in our polyhedron

Spheres of thought
You can just try to have fun
In the masculine expression
As the wave returns
To its point of creation and terminus

The interesting thing
Is how long to keep it all going
And the story you create

The molecule is bound in and out
The salt of the womb and the salt of the beach
The birth of life and the birth of man

The cacophonous pulling away
The music of the water
As it rushes over shells
The echo is the sound of being inside
Venus' clam in the early morning
As you lift wet eyelids in hesitation
Curling up around the dewy pearl
And again the brine
On the lips at eight o'clock AM
As everything goes rushing away

Here we are, displaced

IN AND OUT
Six million
Ceaseless reverberations
Between either shore
Three and a half billion
Pulsing as always from the origin

Yet it's still surprising here. Just as they are

Horse

People will lie
about what they've read
when it's something you've written.
They are throwing a side bet on a longshot horse.

Now, their lame horse runs laps
in the middle of the night
dust glowing on the San Gabriels
the whole world cooling its skin from the day's heat.

It runs against shadows
because it wants to call itself a racer.

IN A SPRING GARDEN, BESIDE A DUSTY ROCK

There are four faces of the cherubim
Just as there are four directions
They can move in any one of them
Without turning their bodies

The meaning of life
My father told me,
Is Love;
But I know now
That isn't true

The meaning of life
Is the appreciation
Of everything:
What most would call nothing,
Only the play of light and shadow

At the very end, art shows us
That every work
Is an act of genius
Every form is a miracle
And all of life is worthy
Of endless contemplation

TIMOTHY BARNETT

The Gin & Tonic

When I'm gone, when I'm gone
I'm gone in age, I'm gone in age
Until I won't remember, until I won't remember
I'm gone in age
Please stay–Please Stay

I heard there's a movie playing back in town
Running away, you and me
We were eighteen,
there was nothing more to see

There's nothing quite like this gin and tonic
For if not, you're weak without it
So let it, let it, let it sink in
Let it sink in

Be who you are, be who you are
And do not change, do not, do not
And so go and be it! Go and be it!
You seek to see
what's happening baby, to you and me.

Oh, I loved you
Oh, I loved you
And I pray that I was enough.

TABLE OF CONTENTS

Introduction
Charles Disney — 3

In a Balsamic Vinaigrette
Timothy Barnett — 8

Aimless With No Idea What To Do With My Life
Isaac Simpson — 9

CAR POEM III
Spencer M de Gauthier-StGermain — 10

NOT LOOKING AT WOMEN ON THE STREET POEM
Spencer M de Gauthier-StGermain — 12

$12
Isaac Simpson — 14

ANOTHER POEM FOR THE TRASH (OR THE NEW YORKER, SAME THING!) XXXVI
Spencer M de Gauthier-StGermain — 16

Finally
Isaac Simpson — 20

Every Perfume Has Something Gross In It
Isaac Simpson   22

Magic Beans
Timothy Barnett   24

At Least Now I Can Listen to the Blues and Good Country Music With a Straight Face
Isaac Simpson   27

Roman St. Clarence
Timothy Barnett   28

STATUS UPDATE
Timothy Barnett   31

A HIDDEN SPELL SCROLL: DOWNTOWN AND FROGTOWN REAL ESTATE POEM
Spencer M de Gauthier-StGermain   32

Interlude 1 - Autopilot
Delicious Tacos   35

Beverly Hills Plebs
Timothy Barnett   42

HOW TO ACHIEVE LIBERATION IN POVERTY
Spencer M de Gauthier-StGermain   47

Make it Stick
Isaac Simpson   48

ALIEN POEM
Spencer M de Gauthier-StGermain   50

hope i nevah fuhget
Timothy Barnett   53

It Popped
Timothy Barnett   54

Worshipping Beauty is a Horrible Mistake
Isaac Simpson   56

Lazy
Isaac Simpson   57

THE CHARMING WAY
Spencer M de Gauthier-StGermain   59

THE DEALING GAME
Spencer M de Gauthier-StGermain   60

Boredome........... ennui
Spencer M de Gauthier-StGermain   62

I'M COLLECTING A CERTAIN TYPE OF FOLLOWER [REWOLLEF FO EPYT NIATREC A GNITCELLOC M'I]
Spencer M de Gauthier-StGermain   64

COPING WITH HER, LUXURIANT FAME
Spencer M de Gauthier-StGermain   66

Interlude 2 - Product Review: Tenga® Easy Beat Egg™ Artificial Vagina, "Silky"
Delicious Tacos   69

idol idyllic.
Timothy Barnett   76

ONCE UPON A TIME IN THE BACK ALLEYS OF RODEO DRIVE
Spencer M de Gauthier-StGermain   78

CULPABILITY POEM
Spencer M de Gauthier-StGermain   82

Truth Will Get You
Isaac Simpson   83

Singing Psalms of Praise to Jean Paul Marat and Alex Jones
Spencer M de Gauthier-StGermain   84

Peck Rd South
Timothy Barnett   86

Mellors
Isaac Simpson   87

What's My Tribe?
Isaac Simpson   88

OH EVERYONE'S DOING RUBBINGS NOW
Spencer M de Gauthier-StGermain   91

BUT WERE THERE EVER ANY TOWERS
Spencer M de Gauthier-StGermain   92

Stray Cat On The Bar-B-Que, Staring At A Hummingbird Hum Over Molding, Orange, Crustaceous Blossoms
Timothy Barnett   94

Oil
Timothy Barnett   98

Untitled Poem
Spencer M de Gauthier-StGermain   100

Interlude 3 - Shit Jobs: McDonald's
Delicious Tacos   103

Traveling
Isaac Simpson   112

Crumtples
Isaac Simpson   114

and of course
Timothy Barnett   115

Mary
Isaac Simpson   117

aluminum horse
Timothy Barnett   118

Death by Goodness
Isaac Simpson   121

Fred, the Poem
Isaac Simpson   122

Anti-Love Poem
Isaac Simpson   124

LSD POEM
Spencer M de Gauthier-StGermain   127

the books are on sale
Timothy Barnett   128

On How to be an Angel (with Wings)
Timothy Barnett   130

DEATH DEATH DEATH DEATH DEATH DEATH DEATH
Spencer M de Gauthier-StGermain   132

SPELL SCROLL: PENGUIN PUBLISHING WILL LOVE IT!
Spencer M de Gauthier-StGermain   133

THE HEART OF DARKNESS IS THE PLACE OF PERFECT PEACE
Spencer M de Gauthier-StGermain   134

Horse
Isaac Simpson   137

IN A SPRING GARDEN, BESIDE A DUSTY ROCK
Spencer M de Gauthier-StGermain 138

The Gin & Tonic
Timothy Barnett 139

www.ingramcontent.com/pod-product-compliance
Lightning Source LLC
Chambersburg PA
CBHW020546030426
42337CB00013B/984